HAMSTER

Douglas Bender

TABLE OF CONTENTS

A Pelican Book

Teaching Tips for Caregivers and Teachers:

Research shows that one of the best ways for students to learn a new topic is to read about it.

Before Reading

- Read the title and predict what the book will be about.
- Read the "Words to Know" and discuss the meaning of each word.
- Read the back cover to see what the book is about.

During Reading

- When a student gets to a word that is unknown, ask them to look at the rest of the sentence to find clues to help with the meaning of the unknown word.
- Motivate students with praise and encouragement.

After Reading

- Discuss the main idea of the book.
- Ask students to give one detail that they learned in the book.

SIGHT WORDS

a
all
big
have
is
like
long
many
run
some
this
to

WORDS TO KNOW

cage

ears

hair

hamster

whiskers

This is a **hamster**.

hamster

All hamsters have **whiskers**.

whiskers

Some hamsters have long **hair**.